CARRIE UNDERWOOD
GREATEST HITS: DECADE #1

Arranged by Dan Coates

Produced by
Alfred Music
P.O. Box 10003
Van Nuys, CA 91410-0003
alfred.com

Printed in USA.

ISBN-10: 1-4706-2697-7
ISBN-13: 978-1-4706-2697-6

Photo credit: *Greatest Hits: Decade #1* Photographer: Jeremy Cowart
Management: Ann Edelblute; The H.Q.

www.carrieunderwood.fm
www.carrieunderwoodofficial.com
www.facebook.com/carrieunderwood
www.twitter.com/carrieunderwood

Some Hearts

CARNIVAL RIDE

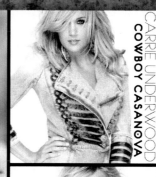

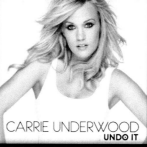
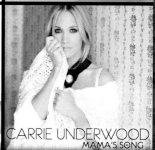

CARRIE UNDERWOOD
COWBOY CASANOVA

CARRIE UNDERWOOD
TEMPORARY HOME

CARRIE UNDERWOOD
UNDO IT

CARRIE UNDERWOOD
MAMA'S SONG

PLAY ON

CARRIE UNDERWOOD
GOOD GIRL

CARRIE UNDERWOOD
BLOWN AWAY

CARRIE UNDERWOOD
TWO BLACK CADILLACS

CARRIE UNDERWOOD

BLOWN AWAY

CONTENTS

—✕—

Something in the Water

Words and Music by Carrie Underwood,
Brett James and Chris DeStefano
Arr. Dan Coates

Verse 2:
Well, I heard what he said and I went on my way,
Didn't think about it for a couple of days.
Then it hit me like lightning late one night,
I was all out of hope, and all out of fight.
Couldn't fight back the tears, so I fell on my knees.
Saying, "God, if You're there, come and rescue me."
Felt love pouring down from above,
Got washed in the water, washed in the blood.
(To Chorus:)

Little Toy Guns

Words and Music by Carrie Underwood,
Hillary Lindsey and Chris DeStefano
Arr. Dan Coates

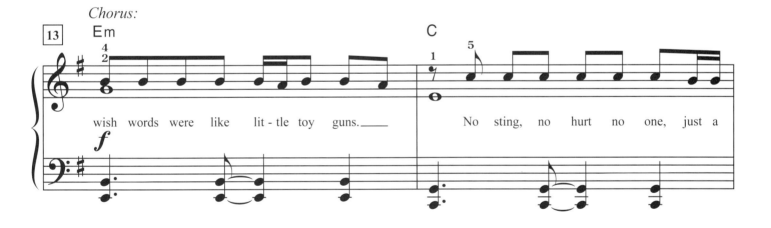

No smoke,___ no bul-lets,___ no kick from the trig-ger when you pull it. No

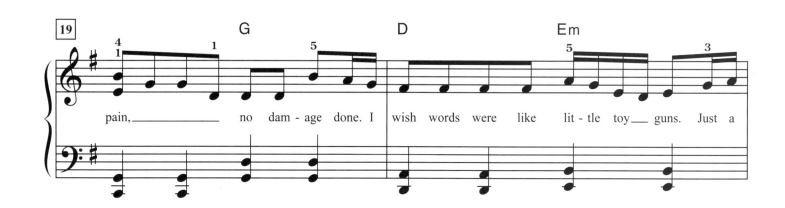

pain,_____ no dam-age done. I wish words were like lit-tle toy___ guns. Just a

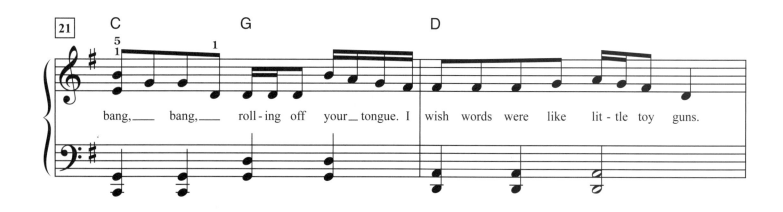

bang,___ bang,___ roll-ing off your___ tongue. I wish words were like lit-tle toy guns.

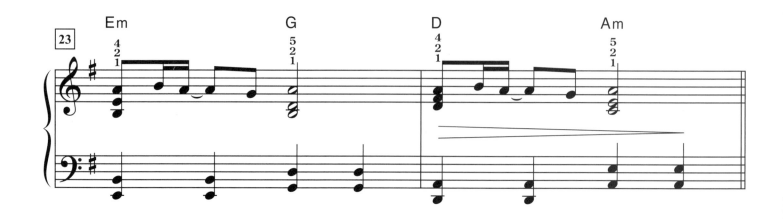

Verse:

2. Wish there was a white flag wav - ing or that they were both just fak - ing, and

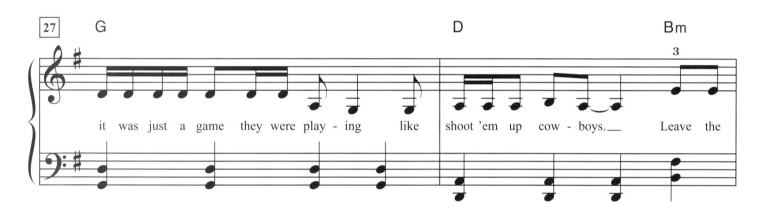

it was just a game they were play - ing like shoot 'em up cow - boys.__ Leave the

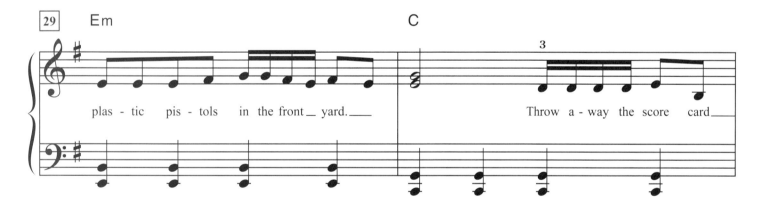

plas - tic pis - tols in the front __ yard. ___ Throw a - way the score card __

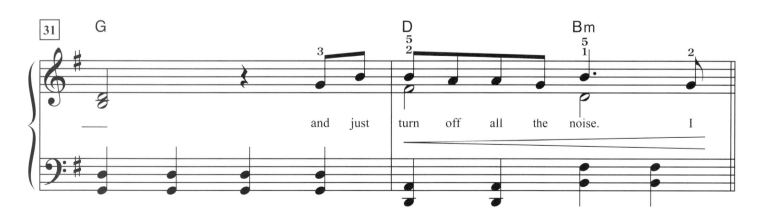

___ and just turn off all the noise. I

Chorus:

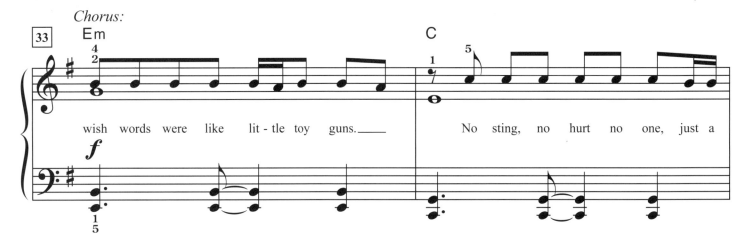

wish words were like lit - tle toy guns.____ No sting, no hurt no one, just a

bang,____ bang____ roll - ing off your tongue. I wish words were like lit - tle toy guns.

No smoke,__ no bul - lets, no kick from the trig - ger when you pull it. No

pain,_____ no dam - age done. I wish words were like lit - tle toy__ guns. Just a

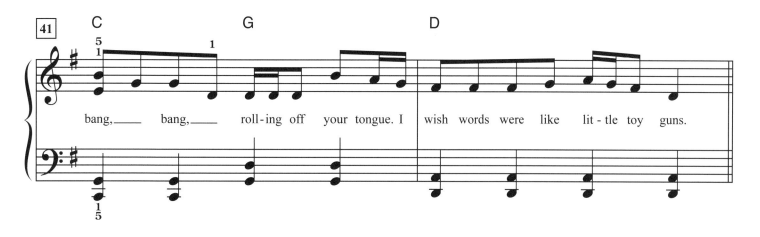

bang,_____ bang,_____ roll-ing off your tongue. I wish words were like lit-tle toy guns.

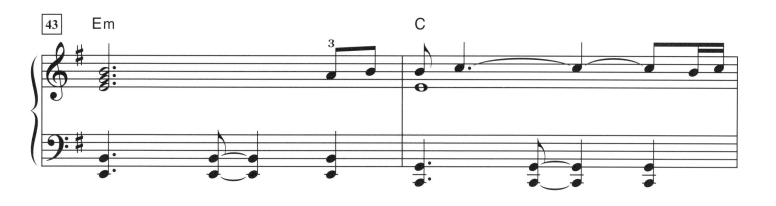

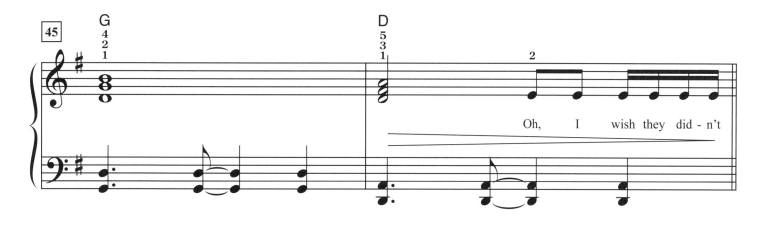

Oh, I wish they did - n't

Bridge:

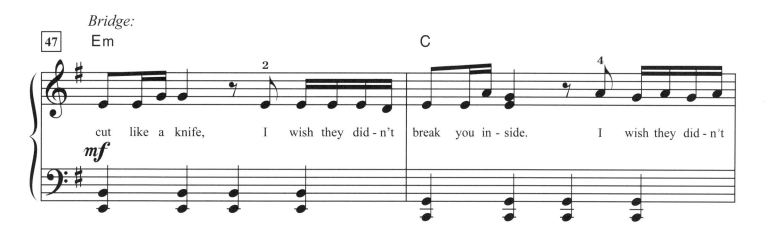

cut like a knife, I wish they did - n't break you in - side. I wish they did - n't

bang,___ bang,___ make you wan - na run,___ yeah.___

Chorus:

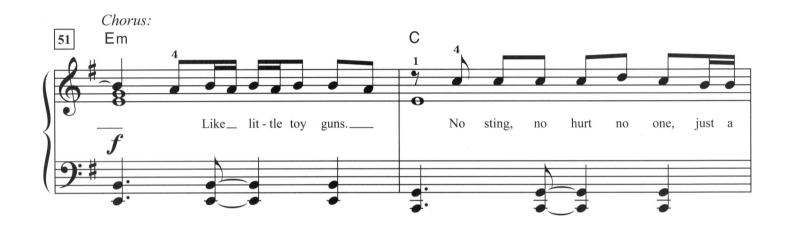

Like__ lit - tle toy guns.___ No sting, no hurt no one, just a

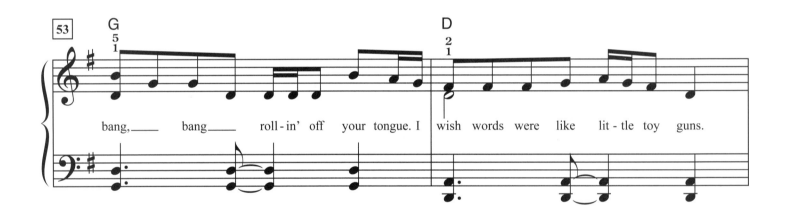

bang,___ bang___ roll - in' off your tongue. I wish words were like lit - tle toy guns.

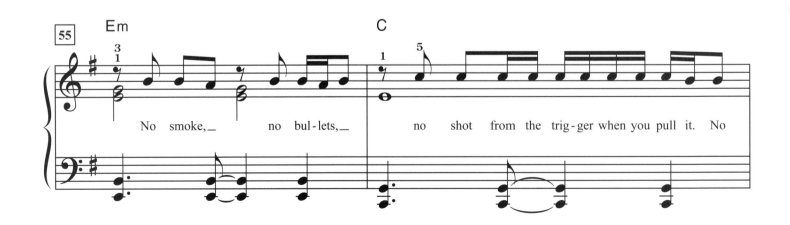

No smoke,__ no bul - lets,__ no shot from the trig - ger when you pull it. No

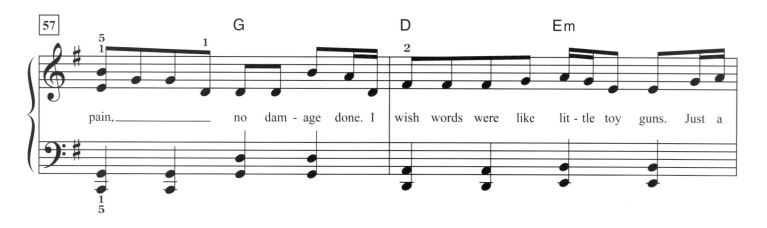

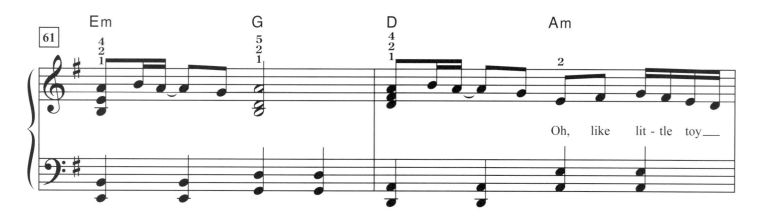

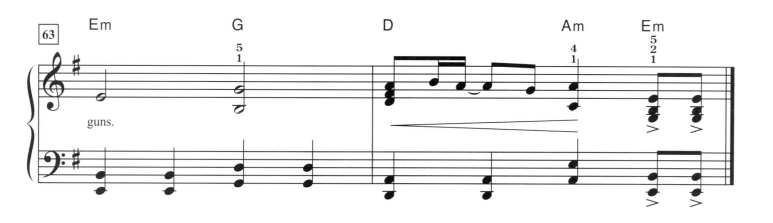

Inside Your Heaven

Words and Music by Per Nylen,
Savan Kotecha and Andreas Carlsson
Arr. Dan Coates

Jesus, Take the Wheel

Words and Music by Brett James,
Gordie Sampson and Hillary Lindsey
Arr. Dan Coates

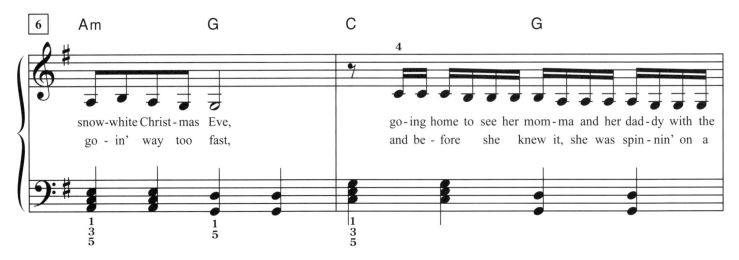

26

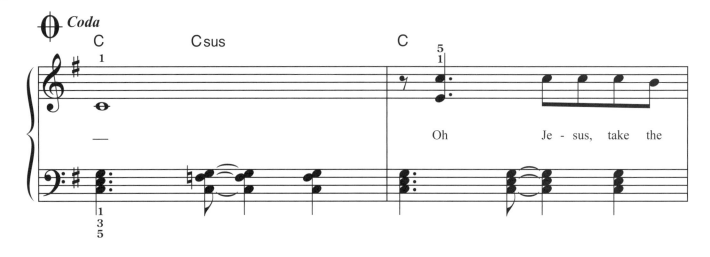

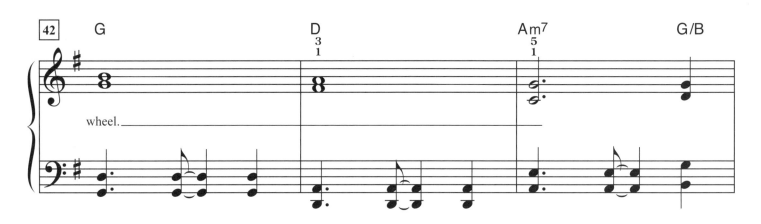

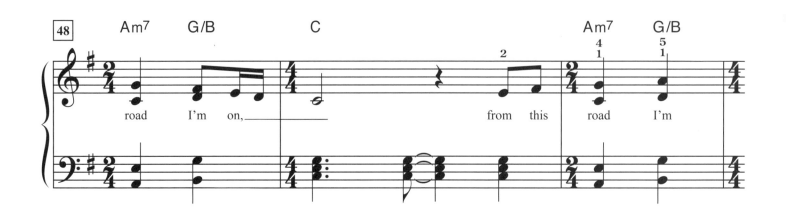

Don't Forget to Remember Me

Words and Music by Morgane Hayes,
Kelley Lovelace and Ashley Gorley
Arr. Dan Coates

Moderately slow

33

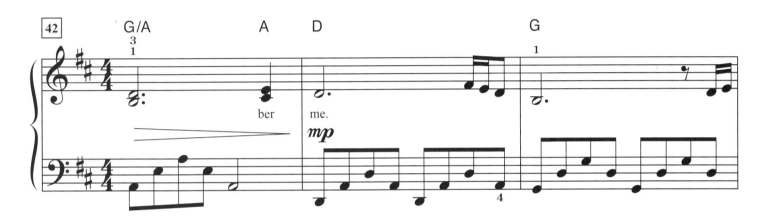

Verse 2:
This downtown apartment sure makes me miss home,
And those bills there on the counter keep tellin' me I'm on my own.
And just like ev'ry Sunday, I called Momma up last night,
And even when it's not, I tell her ev'rything's all right.
Before we hung up, I said, "Hey Momma, don't forget
To tell my baby sister I'll see her in the fall,
And tell Mema that I miss her. Yeah, I should give her a call.
And make sure you tell Daddy that I'm still his little girl.
Yeah, I still feel like I'm where I'm s'posed to be,
But don't forget to remember me."

Before He Cheats

Words and Music by Josh Kear and Chris Tompkins
Arr. Dan Coates

36

Wasted

Words and Music by Marv Green,
Troy Verges and Hillary Lindsey
Arr. Dan Coates

40

Verse 2:
For one split second, she almost turned around,
But that would be like pouring raindrops back into a cloud.
So, she took another step and said,
"I see the way out and I'm gonna take it."
(To Chorus:)

So Small

Words and Music by Carrie Underwood,
Hillary Lindsey and Luke Laird
Arr. Dan Coates

43

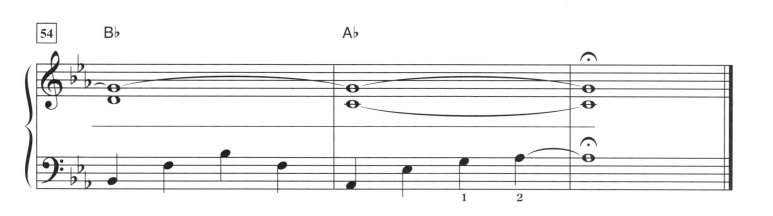

Verse 2:
It's so easy to get lost inside
A problem that seems so big at the time.
It's like a river that's so wide,
It swallows you whole.
While you're sittin' 'round thinkin'
'Bout what you can't change
And worrying about all the wrong things,
Time's flyin' by, movin' so fast.
You better make it count,
'Cause you can't get it back.
(To Chorus:)

46

All-American Girl

Words and Music by Carrie Underwood,
Kelley Lovelace and Ashley Gorley
Arr. Dan Coates

Last Name

Words and Music by Carrie Underwood,
Hillary Lindsey and Luke Laird
Arr. Dan Coates

last name.____ Oh, my ma - ma would be_____ so a -

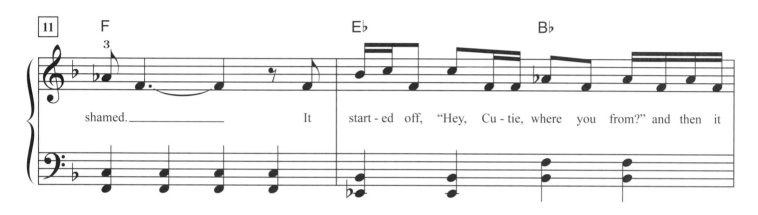

shamed._____ It start - ed off, "Hey, Cu - tie, where you from?" and then it

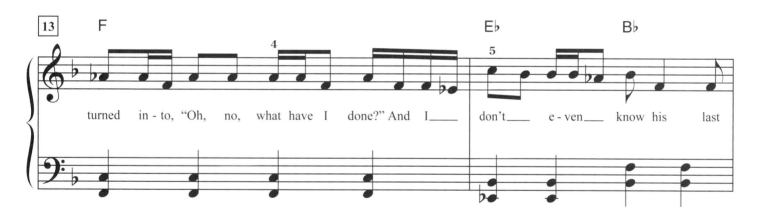

turned in - to, "Oh, no, what have I done?" And I____ don't____ e - ven____ know his last

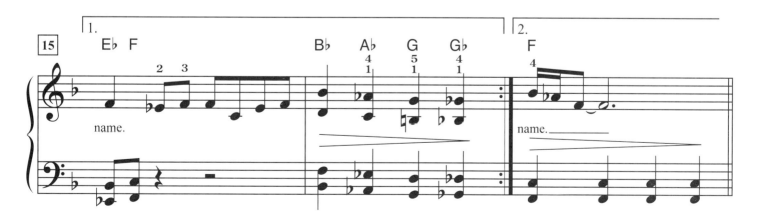

name.   name._____

Verse:

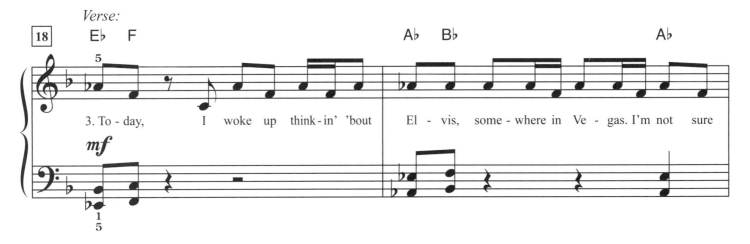

3. To-day, I woke up think-in' 'bout El - vis, some - where in Ve - gas. I'm not sure

how I got here or how this ring on my left hand just ap - peared out of

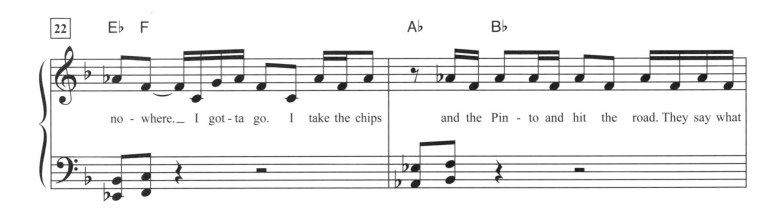

no - where.__ I got-ta go. I take the chips and the Pin - to and hit the road. They say what

hap - pens here,___ stays here,___ all of this - 'll dis - ap - pear.___ I

Verse 2:
We left the club right around three o'clock
In the morning.
His Pinto sittin' there in the parking lot,
Well, it should've been a warning.
I had no clue what I was getting into,
So I blame it on the Cuervo.
(To Chorus:)

Just a Dream

Words and Music by Hillary Lindsey,
Steve McEwan and Gordie Sampson
Arr. Dan Coates

Moderately slow

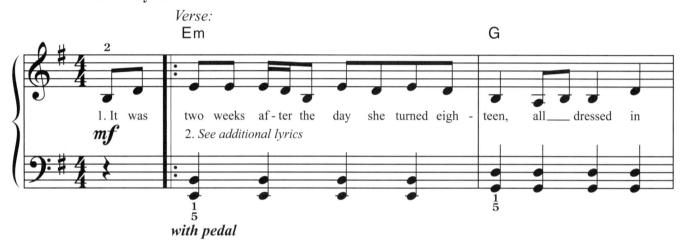

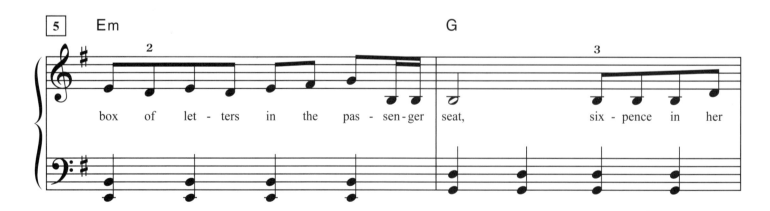

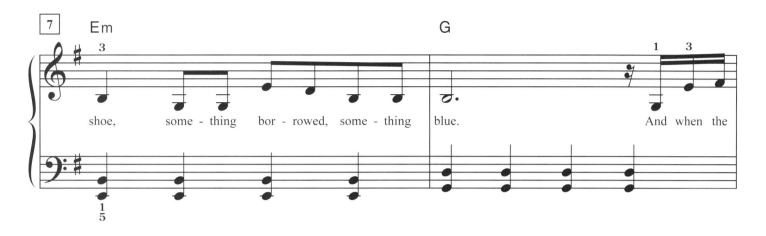

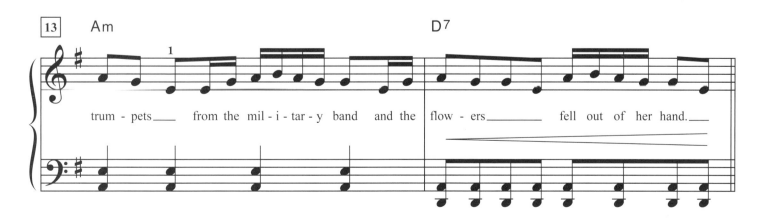

56

Chorus:

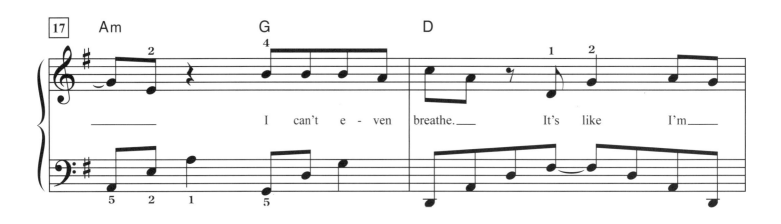

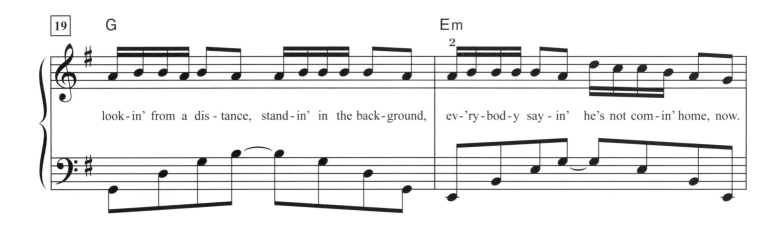

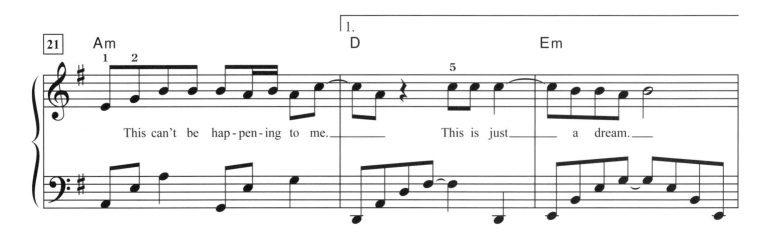

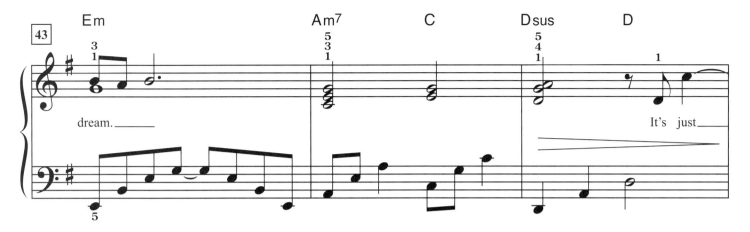

Verse 2:
The preacher man said, "Let us bow our heads and pray.
Lord, please lift his soul and heal this hurt."
Then the congregation all stood up and sang
The saddest song that she ever heard.
And then they handed her a folded-up flag
And she held on to all she had left of him.
Oh, and what could have been.
And then the guns rang one last shot
And it felt like a bullet in her heart.
(To Chorus:)

I Told You So

Words and Music by Randy Travis
Arr. Dan Coates

62

Cowboy Casanova

Words and Music by Carrie Underwood,
Mike Elizondo and Brett James
Arr. Dan Coates

Verse 2:
I see that look on your face.
You ain't hearin' what I say.
So, I'll say it again, 'cause I've been where you been
And I know how it ends, you can't get away, eh.
Don't even look in his eyes.
He'll tell you nothing but lies.
And you wanna believe, but you won't be deceived
If you listen to me and take my advice.
(To Chorus:)

Temporary Home

Words and Music by Carrie Underwood,
Luke Laird and Zac Maloy
Arr. Dan Coates

Verse:

38 C .... F

3. Old man, hos-pi-tal bed, the room is filled with peo-ple he loves.

mp

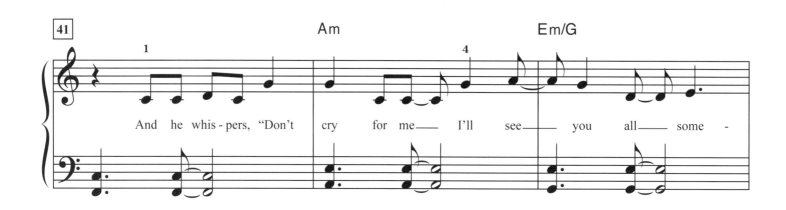

41 .... Am .... Em/G

And he whis-pers, "Don't cry for me I'll see you all some-

44 Fmaj7 .... Am

day." He looks up and says, "I

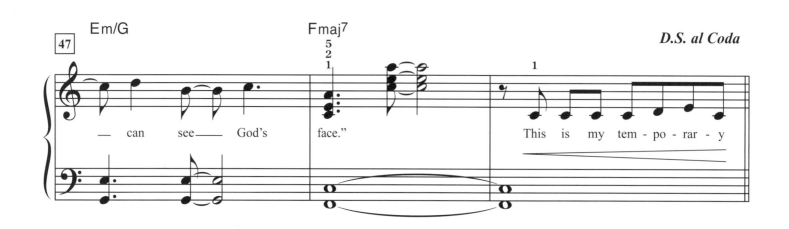

47 Em/G .... Fmaj7 .... *D.S. al Coda*

can see God's face." This is my tem-po-rar-y

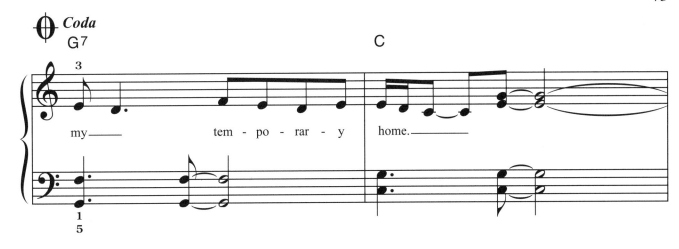

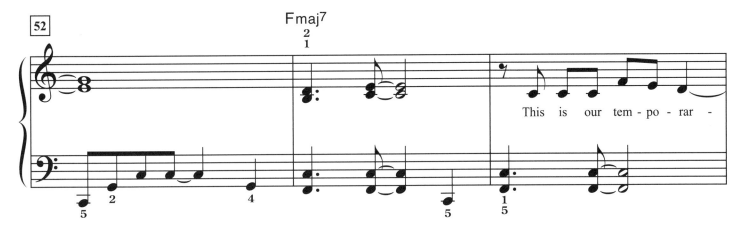

Verse 2:
Young mom on her own,
She needs a little help, got nowhere to go.
She's looking for a job, looking for a way out
'Cause a halfway house will never be a home.
At night she whispers to her baby girl,
Someday we'll find our place here in this world.

Chorus 2:
This is our temporary home,
It's not where we belong.
Windows and rooms that we're passing through.
This is just a stop on the way to where we're going.
I'm not afraid because I know
This is our temporary home.

Undo It

Words and Music by Carrie Underwood,
Kara DioGuardi, Marti Frederiksen and Luke Laird
Arr. Dan Coates

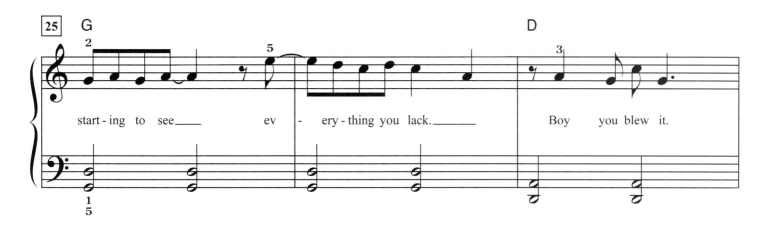

starting to see____ everything you lack.____ Boy you blew it.

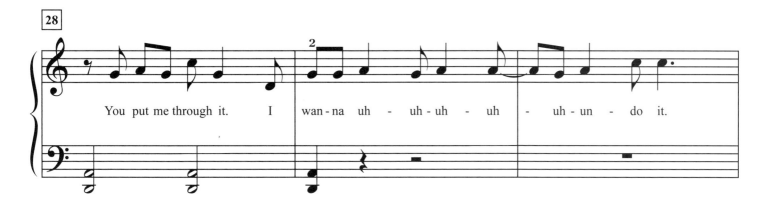

You put me through it. I wanna uh - uh-uh - uh - uh-un - do it.

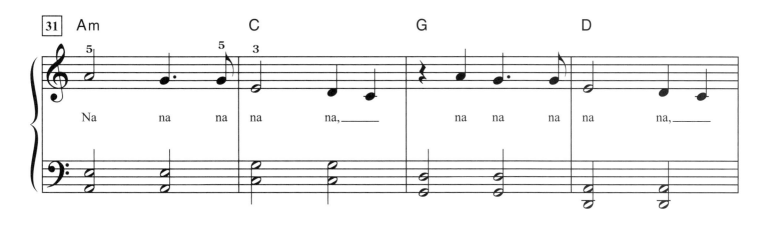

Na na na na na,____ na na na na na,____

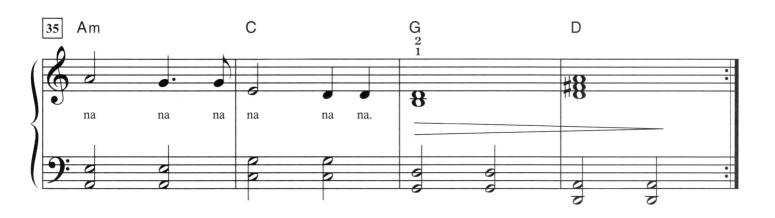

na na na na na na.

78

Mama's Song

Words and Music by Carrie Underwood,
Marti Frederiksen, Kara DioGuardi and Luke Laird
Arr. Dan Coates

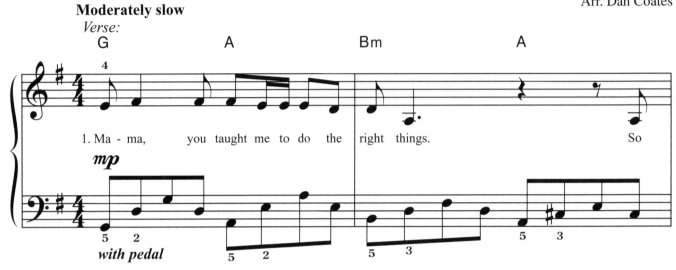

Chorus:

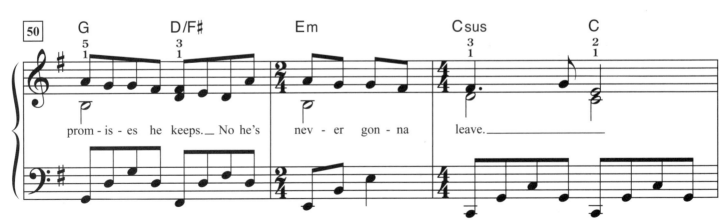

Remind Me

Words and Music by Kelley Lovelace,
Brad Paisley and Chris DuBois
Arr. Dan Coates

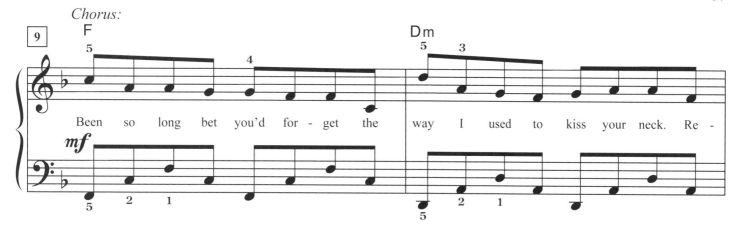

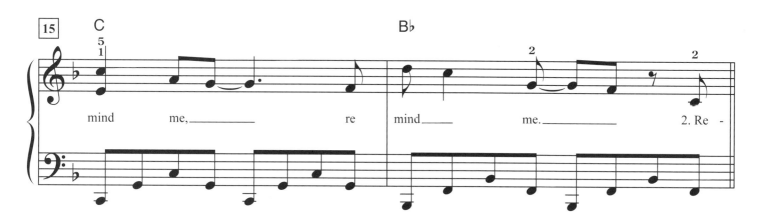

Verse:

mem-ber the air-port, drop-ping me off? We were kiss-ing good-bye and we could-n't stop.

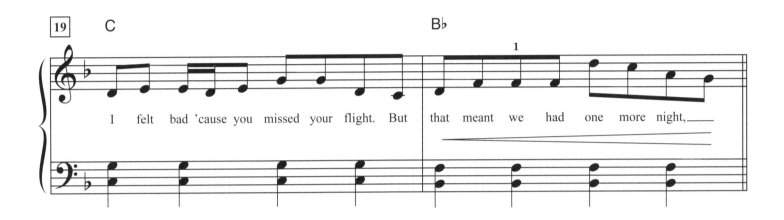

I felt bad 'cause you missed your flight. But that meant we had one more night,____

Chorus:

Do you re-mem-ber how it used to be? We'd turn out the lights and we did-n't just sleep. Re-

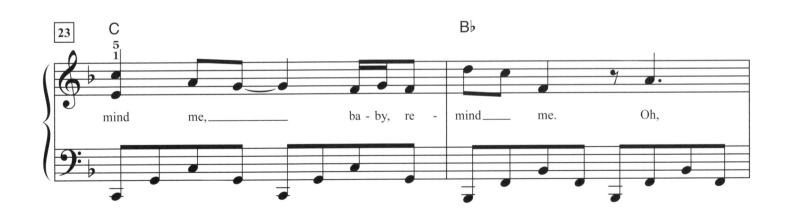

mind me,_____ ba-by, re - mind____ me. Oh,

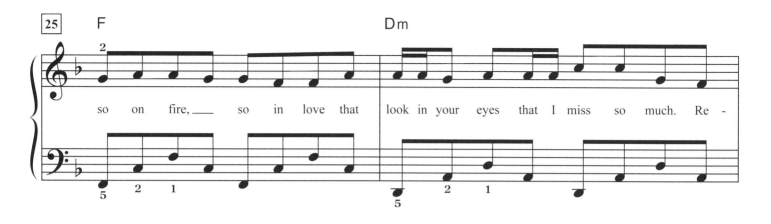

Bridge:

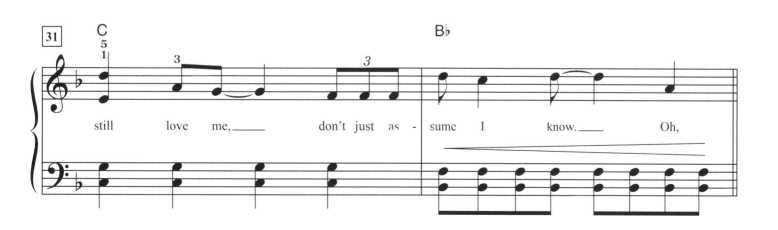

Chorus:

do you re - mem - ber the way it felt? You mean back when we could-n't con - trol our - selves. Re -

mind me,_____ re - mind____ me._____

All those things that you used to do that made____ me fall in__ love with you._ Re -

mind me,_____ re - mind____ me._____

Good Girl

Words and Music by Carrie Underwood,
Ashley Gorley and Chris DeStefano
Arr. Dan Coates

Moderately, with a country rock beat

92

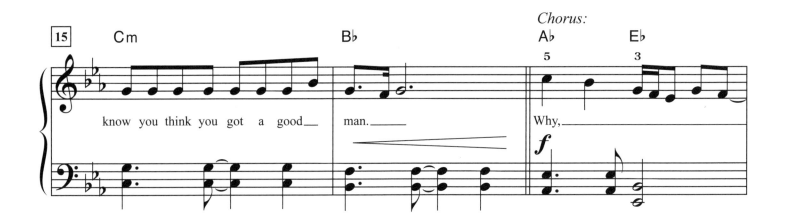

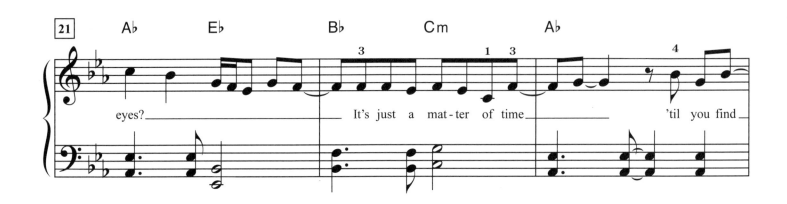

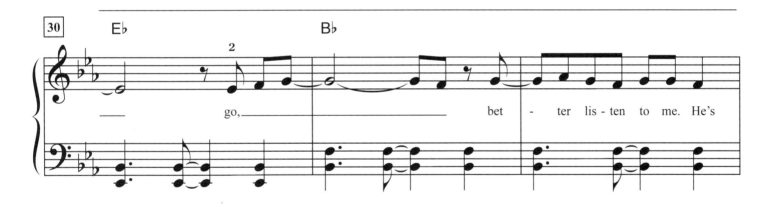

94

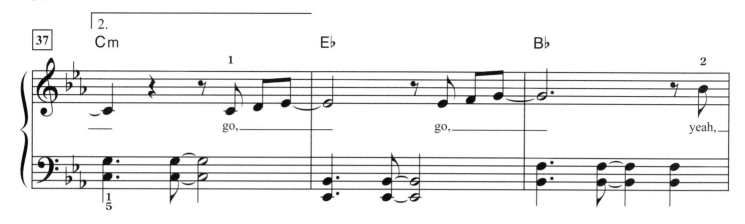

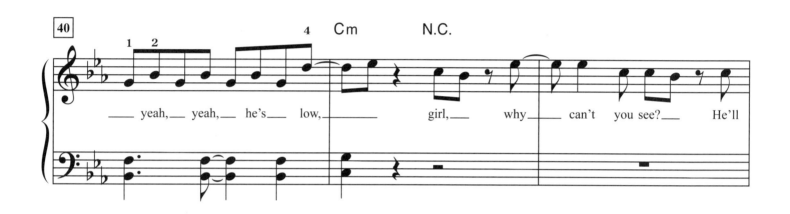

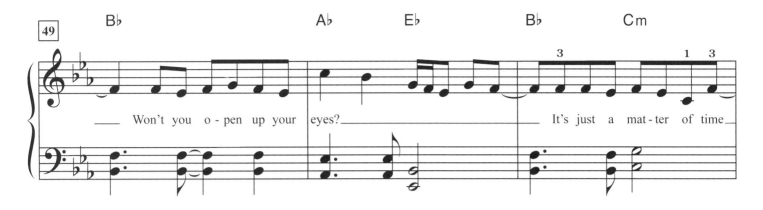

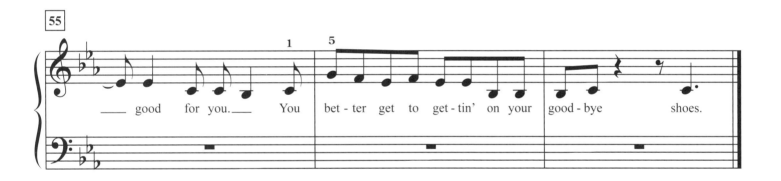

Verse 2:
Hey, good girl, you got a heart of gold,
You want a white wedding and a hand you can hold.
Just like you should, girl, like ev'ry good girl does,
Want a fairy tale ending, somebody to love.
But he's really good at lyin', yeah, he'll leave you in the dust,
'Cuz when he says forever, well, it don't mean much.
Hey, good girl, too good for him.
Better back away, honey, you don't know where he's been.
(To Chorus:)

Blown Away

Words and Music by Josh Kear and Chris Tompkins
Arr. Dan Coates

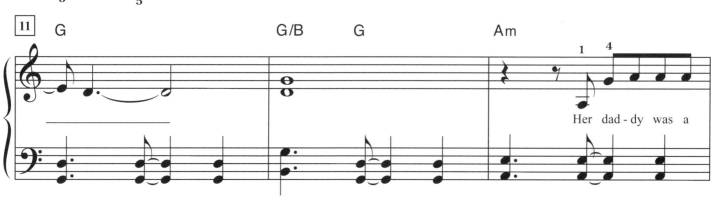

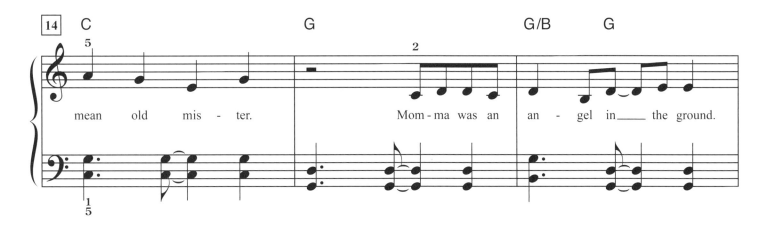

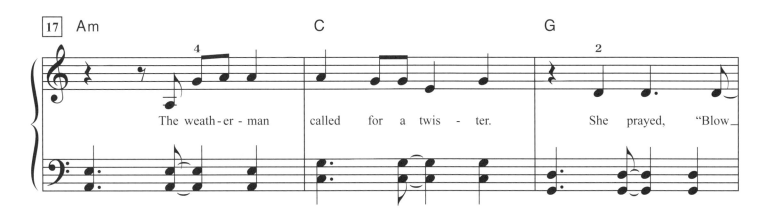

1st time only

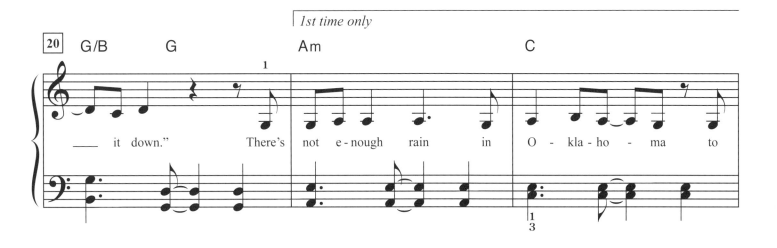

98

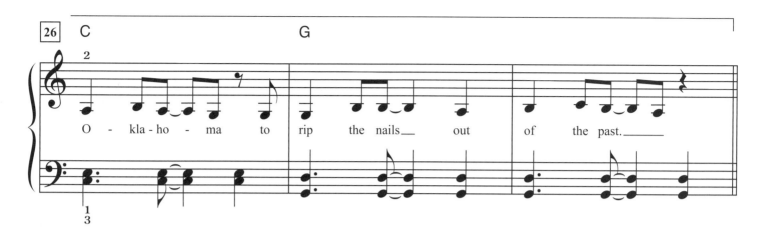

Chorus:

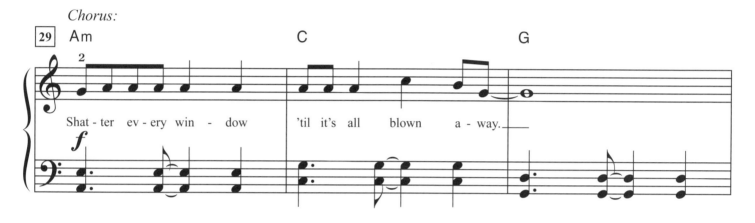

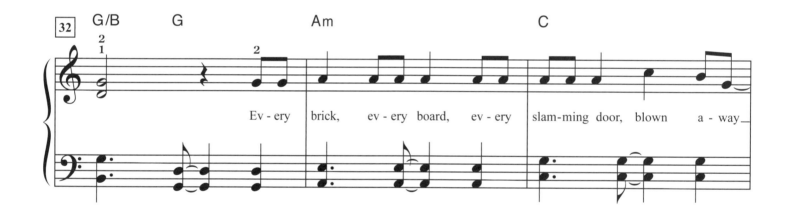

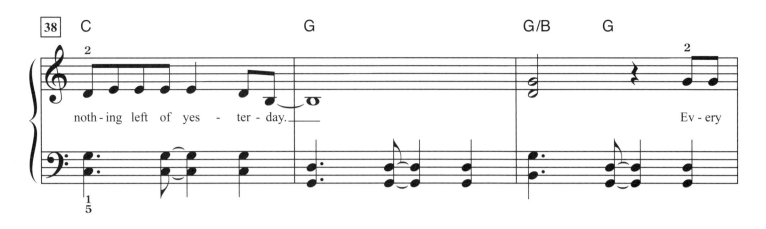

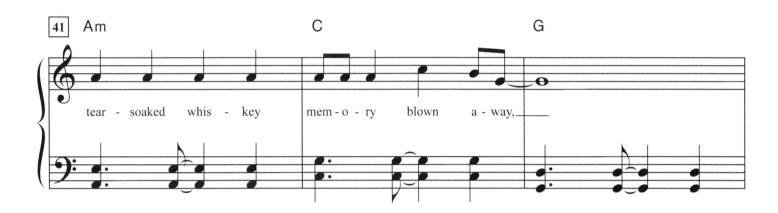

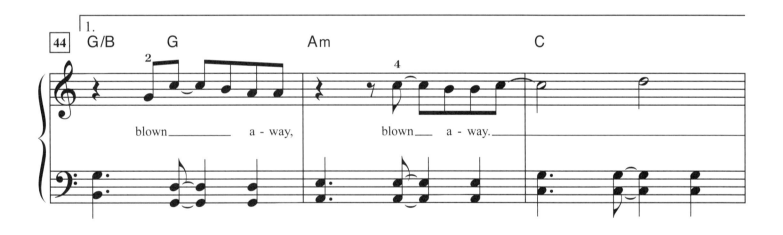

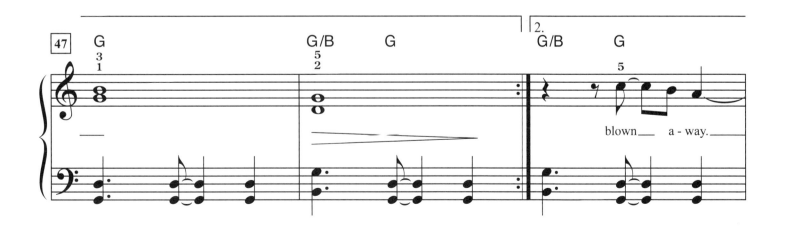

Verse 2:
She heard those sirens screaming out.
Her daddy laid there passed out on the couch.
She locked herself in the cellar,
Listened to the screaming of the wind.
Some people call it taking shelter;
She called it sweet revenge.
(To Chorus:)

Two Black Cadillacs

Words and Music by Carrie Underwood,
Josh Kear and Hillary Lindsey
Arr. Dan Coates

Verse 2:
Two months ago,
His wife called the number on his phone.
Turns out he'd been lying to both of them
For oh, so long.
They decided then he'd never get away
With doing this to them.
Two black Cadillacs waiting for the right time,
The right time.
(To Chorus:)

See You Again

Words and Music by Carrie Underwood,
David Hodges and Hillary Lindsey
Arr. Dan Coates

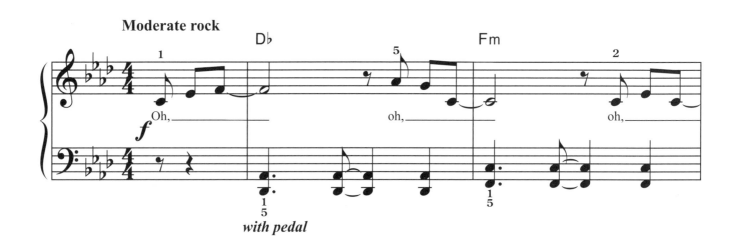

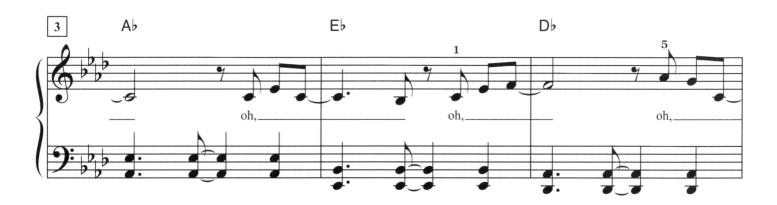

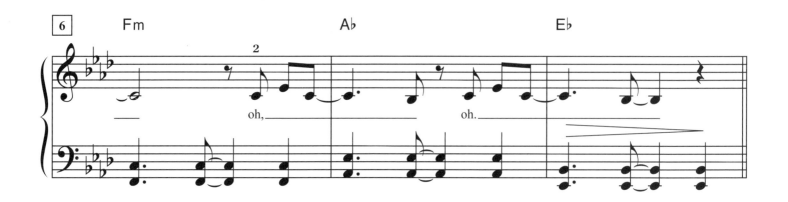

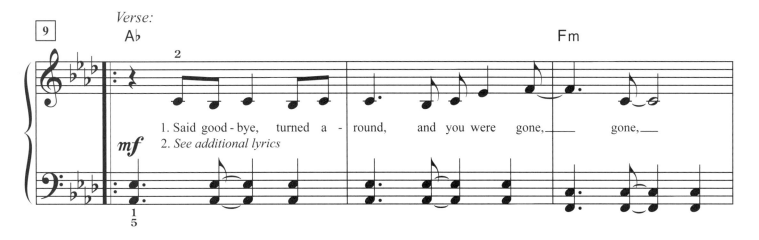

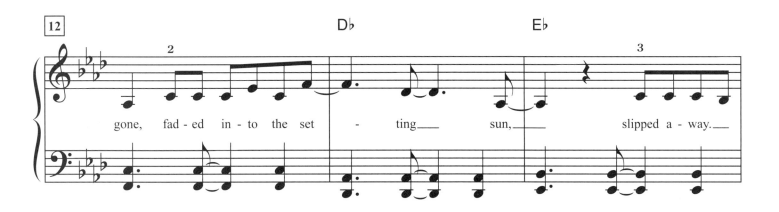

Chorus:

I___ fol - low.___ I will see you a - gain,

___ whoa.___ This is not where it ends.___ I will car -

ry you___ with___ me, oh,___ 'til I see you a - gain.

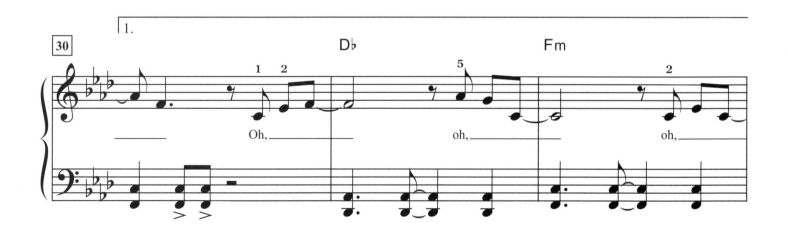

___ Oh,___ oh,___ oh,

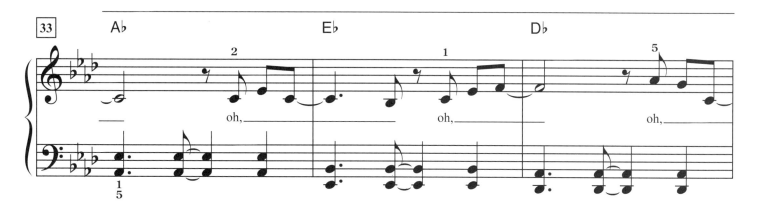

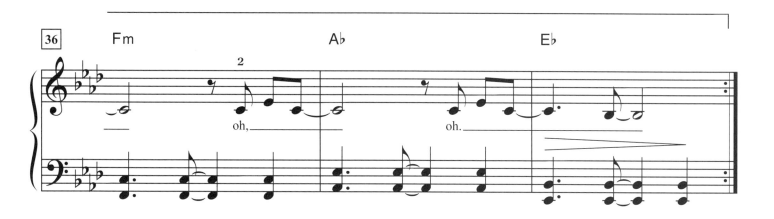

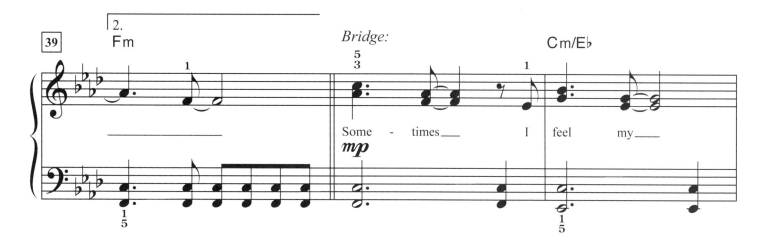

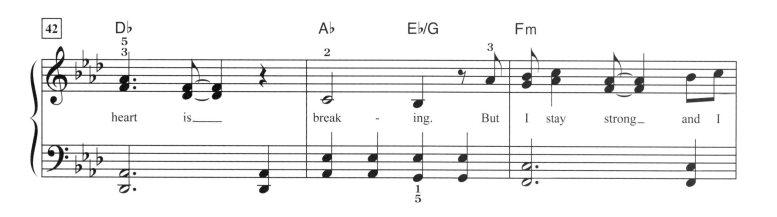

hold_____ on_____ 'cuz I know..._____

I will see you a-gain,_____ whoa._____ This is not where it ends.

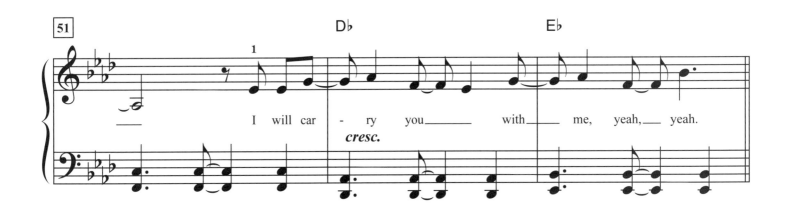

I will car - ry you_____ with____ me, yeah,___ yeah.

I will see you a-gain,_____ whoa,_____ This is not where it ends.

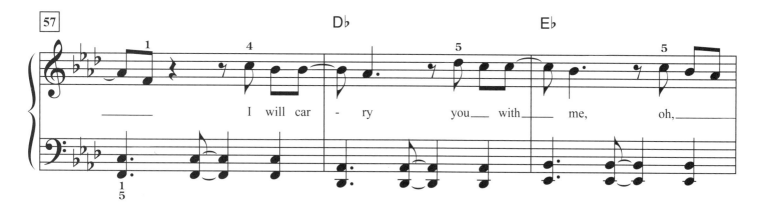

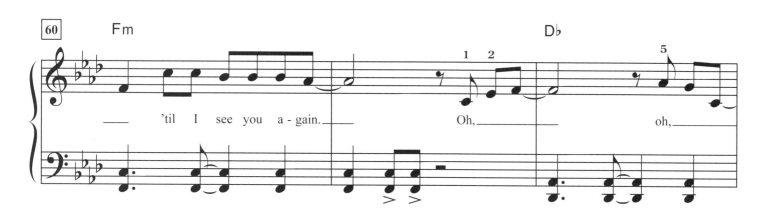

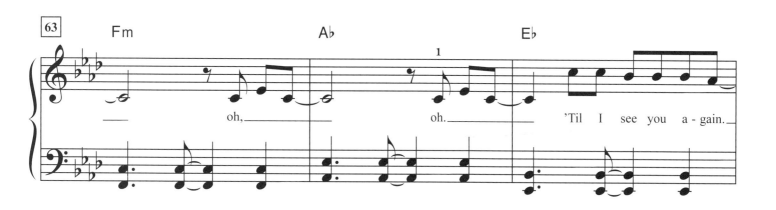

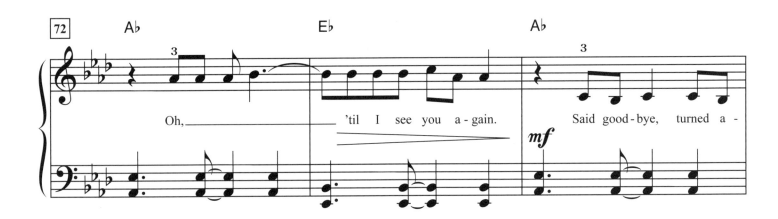

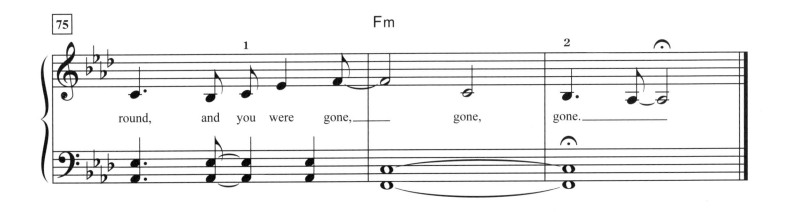

Verse 2:
I can hear those echoes in the wind at night
Calling me back in time, back to you
In a place far away where the water meets the sky.
The thought of it makes me smile.
You are my tomorrow.
(To Chorus:)

How Great Thou Art

Words and Music by Stuart K. Hine
Arr. Dan Coates

114

115

Verse 2:
When Christ shall come,
With shout of acclamation,
And take me home, what joy shall fill my heart!
Then I shall bow,
In humble adoration,
And then proclaim:
"My God, how great Thou art!"
(To Chorus:)